P.B. BEAR'S

WORLD OF WORDS

Lee Davis

Family Learning

HOW TO USE THIS BOOK

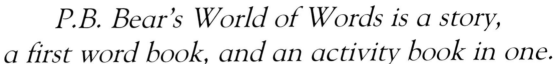

*P.B. Bear's World of Words is a story,
a first word book, and an activity book in one.*

Children will love the story of P.B. Bear's balloon ride.
As you read it out loud, they will enjoy matching the
objects in the borders to those in the main pictures
– increasing their vocabulary as they do so.

Each picture is packed with delightful details.
The activity questions can be used as a starting
point for enjoying the pictures, and as a tool to
help children develop their observation skills.

Don't forget to look out for the little bear.

Which pages
can you find
me on?

P.B. BEAR'S DAY

slippers

robe

pants

shirt

cap

pajamas

shorts

jeans

sandals

"I have a feeling that this is going to be a very busy day," says P.B. Bear one morning. "What shall I wear?"

4

wardrobe

chest of drawers

socks

handkerchief

underwear

vest

scarf

hat

shoes

sweater

Can you point to some of P.B. Bear's clothes that are

 yellow 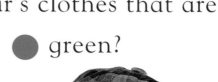 blue red green?

overalls

T-shirt

rain hat

boots

5

schoolbag

purse

zipper

umbrella

raincoat

sponge

soap dish

soap

hairbrush

cup

water

mirror

sea horse

bubble bath

towel

bathtub

back brush

"I have an idea for an adventure," says P.B. Bear
"But I've got a lot to do first!"
P.B. Bear washes his face and brushes his teeth.
"Now I'm ready to start my busy day!" he says.

faucets

comb

washcloth

cotton balls

rubber duck

nail brush

plug

tissues

shampoo

🦆 How many bears can you find in P.B. Bear's bathroom?

🦆 How many different brushes can you see?

7

sink

toothbrush

toothpaste

cotton swabs

sofa

table

pillows

marbles

lamp

clock

toy boat

drawing

"I'm making something special," says P.B. Bear. "Can you guess what it is? It will fly, but it's not an airplane or a space rocket!"

- What can you see that makes music?
- What can you see that is used for coloring pictures?

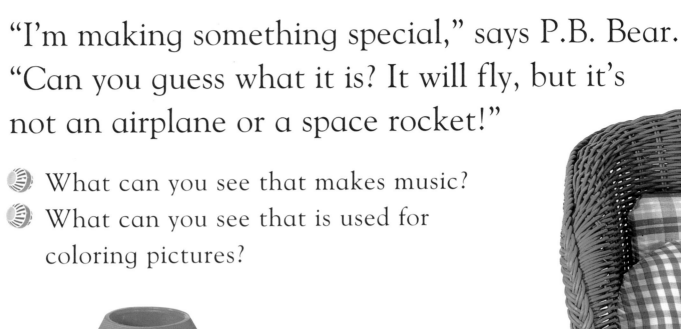

paint

paintbrushes

scissors

crayons

toy car

playing cards

jigsaw puzzle

drum

horn

blocks

basket

9

colored pencils

ball

toy mouse

balloon

watering can

basket

daffodils

butterflies

caterpillar

garden rake

trowel

broom

garden fork

P.B. Bear has made a hot-air balloon that will take him on a high-flying adventure. "Ready for takeoff," he says. "Good-bye backyard!"

10

flowerpot

seeds

clippers

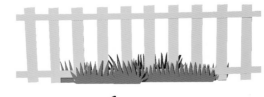
fence

snail

ant

potatoes

heads of lettuce

bean plants

Can you find...

- 1 bird
- 2 butterflies
- 3 heads of lettuce
- 4 daffodils
- 5 ants?

carrots

tomatoes

tree

bird

hot-air balloon

11

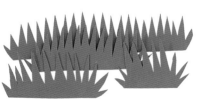
grass

binoculars

camera

hot-air balloon

tent

fence

cloud

mountains

well

windmill

tractor

trailer

12

farmhouse

barn

bridge

train

village

rabbit

ducklings

duck

cow

The balloon drifts above the countryside.
The animals on the ground look very small.
Can you help P.B. Bear spot...

Which animal is crossing the bridge?
Which animal is perched on the fence?

goose

pig

sheep

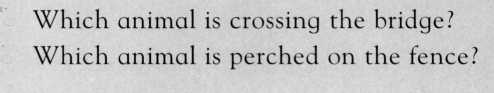

rooster

13

cat

horse

frog

bird

chicken

hat

sunglasses

towel

postcards

pencil

sunblock

sandwich

Bob

Roscoe

Dermott

Next, the balloon travels toward the seashore and lands on the beach.
"Ahoy there, sailors!" P.B. Bear calls out to some friends.

14

fish

dolphins

starfish

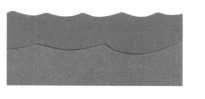
sea

pebbles

rock

seagull

Can you find these shapes at the seashore?

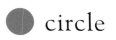 circle   star   rectangle

 square 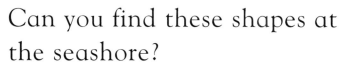 triangle

lighthouse

boat

sand castle

15

spade

sand

seaweed

shells

bucket

waiter

police officer

nurse

firefighter

office worker

bicycle

airplane

bus

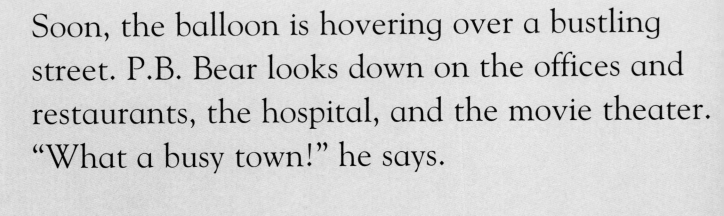

Soon, the balloon is hovering over a bustling street. P.B. Bear looks down on the offices and restaurants, the hospital, and the movie theater. "What a busy town!" he says.

chair

table

movie theater

hospital

car

motorcycle

fire engine

mail carrier

mailbox

road sign

traffic light

How many nurses can you see?
How many waiters can you see?
How many firefighters can you see?

RESTAURANT

HOSPITAL

OFFICE

restaurant

supermarket

café

office building

flower seller

sun

pond

bee

grasshopper

trees

tree house

bench

slide

jump rope

 What is Franny doing?
 What is Dixie doing?
 What is Milly doing?

18

seesaw

swing

skateboard

ladybug

lunch box

backpack

Franny

Then P.B. sees some friends in the playground.
"Stop and play with us," they call.
B$_{U}$MP goes the balloon on the seesaw,
before lifting back up into the air.
"I can't stop now!" says P.B. Bear.
"It's suppertime!"

Dixie

Hilda

Milly

19

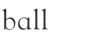

ball

paddles

hoop

Russell

orange juice

butter

bowl

carrots

celery

honey

bread

ice cream

plates

A gentle breeze blows the balloon back home. "All that traveling has made me hungry!" says P.B. Bear.

mugs

salt and pepper

dishwashing liquid

cupboard

 breadsticks

 grapes

 apple

 lemon

 cereal

 spaghetti

Look at the things to eat in P.B. Bear's kitchen.

- Which are hot? Which are cold?
- Which are sweet? Which are sour?
- Which are hard? Which are soft?

 toaster

 brush

 dustpan

 knife fork spoon

 kettle

 saucepan

 stove

table

rug

flashlight

friends

lamp

clock

notebook

pen

22

diary

shoes

binoculars

slippers

photographs

camera

telescope

vase

"It **has** been a busy day and now I'm very sleepy," yawns P.B. Bear.
"Good night."

Can you remember all the words in P.B. Bear's world?

daffodils

curtains

moon

window

book

comforter

stars

bed

Where in the world of words would you like to go?

FAMILY LEARNING

Designers Claire Jones, Jeanette Evans, Claire Ricketts
Editors Caryn Jenner, Fiona Munro   **US Editor** Kristin Ward
Photography Dave King   **Illustration** Judith Moffatt
Production Katy Holmes   **DTP Design** Kim Browne

First American Edition, 1998
4 6 8 10 9 7 5 3

Published in the United States by
DK Publishing, Inc., 375 Hudson Street,
New York, New York 10014

Library of Congress Cataloging-in-Publication Data
Davis, Lee, 1941–
P.B. Bear's World of Words / Lee Davis. — 1st American ed.
p.   cm.
Summary: The reader is asked to identify objects and answer activity questions
related to P.B. Bear's balloon ride.
ISBN 0-7894-3109-2
1. Vocabulary—Juvenile literature   [1. Vocabulary.]   I. Title.
PE1449.D335   1998
428.1—dc21   97-44424
                                                                          CIP
                                                                          AC

Reproduced in Italy by G.R.B. Editrice
Printed and bound in Italy by L.E.G.O.

Acknowledgments
DK would like to thank the following
manufacturers for permission to photograph copyright material:
Ty Inc. for "Toffee" the dog and "Freddie" the frog;
Folkmanis Inc. for the hen puppet;
The Manhattan Toy Company for "Antique Rabbit."

DK would also like to thank:
Maggie Haden, Richard Blakey, Vera Jones, and Barbara Owen

Did you find the little bear on pages 5, 6, 8, 10, 15, 20 and 23?